David Deutsch did not know he would travel this far in writing but is anxious to see where it all goes from here. Apart from writing, he loves watching movies, telling jokes, and exercising.

As far as a life philosophy, he believes we should listen first, think second, speak last and not worry so much about being right since 'incorrect is not the same as ignorant.'

For Cecilia

David Deutsch

Poetsy II

More Poetry
Inspired by Cecilia

AUSTIN MACAULEY PUBLISHERS™

LONDON • CAMBRIDGE • NEW YORK • SHARJAH

Ordering Information
Quantity sales: Special discounts are available on quantity purchases by corporations, associations, and others. For details, contact the publisher at the address below.

Publisher's Cataloging-in-Publication data
Deutsch, David
Poetsy II

ISBN 9798889102694 (Paperback)
ISBN 9798889102717 (ePub e-book)
ISBN 9798889102700 (Audiobook)

Library of Congress Control Number: 2022917381

www.austinmacauley.com/us

First Published 2024
Austin Macauley Publishers LLC
40 Wall Street, 33rd Floor, Suite 3302
New York, NY 10005
USA

mail-usa@austinmacauley.com
+1 (646) 5125767

I hope my appreciation is already felt by that long list of people (too long to write here) who have encouraged me to this point by making me feel like a real author.

This book is a continuation of my previous book; *Poetsy*. It starts from where the previous book ended i.e. chapter 51.

51.

When kindest melodies and lyrics came
To my ears, at once your image appeared
In mind, and suddenly my legs went lame,
The song replaced by thoughts of my endeared;
Because your sight is like a symphony
Of cherubim, who sing at God's footstools.
Your voice, too, rivals diamonds' brilliancy,
Rend'ring mine mute, my mind made as a fool's;
So when things of beauty, joy, and laughter
Present themselves to me at any time,
Know the thought of you will soon come after,
Making each good thing all the more sublime.
And yes, even those things in life so rough
Are endurable now, for you're enough.

52.

You, smile-maker, cause joy so glorious
It cannot be hidden by any mask,
Melting thickest veils with light rays furious,
Like those in which hottest desert sands bask.
Nor can this joy be jailed by etiquette-
The silly rules that mock love's expression.
Formality's calm can't make me forget
My joy when you made your first impression.
And no, neither can the powers of space
And time block the brightness of this feeling.
Miles and years apart cannot encase
Such bliss as has me thankfully kneeling.
My own fear that I'm nothing but a boy
Is all that could ever hold back this joy.

53.

I do not care if you hold the record
For most flaws held by a single person
Or if your past is for sure most checkered
And people know you only for your sin;
For if you are a checker board, the square
I know is the most flawless square on earth.
If you have other ones that aren't as fair,
They surely still cannot demean your worth.
Check to see – prove it to yourself and me:
Challenge my love with your worst confession.
Truth comes after the promise of mercy,
While fear of judgment halts truth's expression.
When made to strive then love is at its best-
An active caring not inclined to rest.

54.

Being in love is how I learned to sing-
No monocle-wearing tutor did this.
I can't learn to thread a needle with string,
But I know the method of daily bliss.
Every time my voice takes on this doing,
A fleshless piece of you enters the air,
And without knowing, you start renewing
Every stranger's spirit who stops to stare.
My song is but the sound of your mem'ry,
The sound of all good things on earth at once.
Your music can make silk out of em'ry
And a mind of wisdom out of a dunce.
And so I think, "Who could ever sing well
Who didn't first feel love that wouldn't quell?"

55.

If I never learn to accept you're gone,
At least I'll think each day of something good.
I'll give you my idolatry each dawn,
Even if I lose my chance at sainthood.
If this longing for you never ceases,
At least it will not be for any drug
But for medicine that health increases,
Though it will not again enter my mug.
There's so much evil that could possess me
That I'm grateful to be taken early
By a clean and friendly spirit of glee
Who wipes out all things that make me surly.
What occupies me here is no demon
But a master who makes me a free man.

56.

While others from my past haunt me as ghosts,
Your ling'ring presence is like an angel.
You make me feel guarded by heaven's hosts.
Others make me feel cursed by imps of hell.
Theirs are the souls of zombies and corpses;
But yours is the soul celestials covet.
Even they have not known one so gorgeous;
But bugs from hell cause me pain and love it.
What pain me most are the words of others.
Your mouth is the top of a waterfall
Of encouragement that gently smothers.
As fists hurt face, words nab a soul to maul.
I will not give the conclusion to them
But to you who makes this dud feel a gem.

57.

There's one whose great power softens my fears,
Whose strength of magic and might does not scare.
Whether she lifts mansions or outwits seers,
I need not feel insecure or beware.
It's true I distrust and dislike power
For the creator of suff'ring it is,
And there's nothing I can do to wow her-
Her skills flare with fire while mine fizz-
But there are exceptions to most all rules
(And exceptional is her way for sure),
So in this, I'll embrace power like jewels
And treat it not as cancer but as cure.
With her, there is no shame in looking weak,
Because through her my heart has reached its peak.

58.

You are the damn I give, and what a dam
You are to hold back such floods of anguish;
And to think, though less vicious than a lamb,
You bear the strength to do all that you wish.
It seems you wish to keep from me dark thoughts.
For your barrier, I am most grateful,
Since it protects me from grief's arrow shots
And from anger's fantasies most hateful.
As Jupiter shelters earth from comets,
So you shield my mind from mental debris.
I weakly absorb others' words like hits
And find it hard with others to agree.
You're the exception I wish were the rule
And the cover for a mental cesspool.

59.

Now I know why Ludwig wrote *Ode to Joy:*
Clearly, Beethoven had you on his mind.
Though how you traversed time… Oh, you're so coy!
I'm sure he grieved when you left him behind.
A grand masterpiece like symphony nine
Has no other possible origin.
The composer met you and saw you shine,
For no influence is to you akin.
It is harder to explain its splendor
Without you than to explain the time skip.
There is simply no other contender
To account for such flawless craftsmanship
Will you jump time again for me before
I die to make my final days less sore?

60.

The one I love is someone with no kind.
No category can hold her luster.
Her glow's too bright for all types I can find,
Defying sort, species, breed, and cluster.
As God creates, but obeys not, nature,
So this one makes the rules of attraction,
Acting as her own high legislature,
While her scoffers only add subtraction.
In short, she can never be called "one of."
About her, this one truth is the clearest.
No tongue's description fits her like a glove,
But the happiest of words come nearest.
Type works to bind me in limitation.
She sits above any imitation.

61.

Is it unfair that love's not hard with you?
I hear others' stories of love's hardships,
How disappointment hurts not just a few,
Making lovers restrain arms and guard lips.
I know, too, I did nothing deserving.
This is all your doing, all your credit.
I benefit from your grace unswerving.
Like children who vast fortunes inherit.
Can it be unfair but still a good thing?
Something that requires no forgiveness?
Yes. I will not suffer a guilty sting,
But show sympathy for them who live less.
Thanksgiving for and to you I provide,
And prayer for them whose pains are magnified.

62.

I will hold myself to standards unreal
And tell you not to do a single thing;
And you will likely do the same, I feel,
Telling me to rest while you're enduring.
I do not mind working hard for you, boss.
To strive long for my own self-worth: that's hard.
If you're not here to watch, my gain is loss,
Accomplishment's satisfaction is marred.
Though your love is grace, still I want to earn.
I want to say your affection's my right,
But no merit allows me to be stern
And deny you the freedom to take flight.
If while young men, we march to peaks above,
Girls we like will be the women we love.

63.

When I felt the want to write about you,
But could not think of the rhymes I needed,
I went to others' art to find a clue
But found nothing fit, for I had cheated;
For only I have ever felt this force-
Unlike gravity, magnetic, nuclear-
That's stronger than life, with you as its source,
A force that regards not powers or years.
It's obvious English now needs new words.
Since your birth, its best lines do not cut it.
We'll make a new language from the songbirds,
And with your wisest sayings we'll glut it.
Until that new and better tongue is found,
Please accept my English rhyming love sound.

64.

The bard composed one hundred fifty-four.
Such was the limit of what inspired him;
But I believe I can compose far more
With the inspiration with which I brim.
Whoever moved William to rhyme his words
Could not have been your equal in brightness.
You could coax a loner to live in herds
Or a drunken jerk to learn politeness.
Yes, you can draw out from me more sonnets,
For your silent persuasion is matchless.
You could turn green the bluest bluebonnets
And soften the angriest no to yes.
Your memory allows my soul to thrive,
So I can make one hundred fifty-five.

65.

My love is nothing but neurons evolved?
Nature's way of propagating lifeforms?
The secret of my spirit has been solved:
Love's simply a gene that nat'ral strife forms.
If that's the cause behind love, so be it!
Explanation does not reduce meaning.
My love has worth because I decree it,
Without nature or God intervening.
Whether love consists of cells or soul bits,
Its value and effects remain the same.
Still it shines with the starriest of glitz.
Still it moves me to risk the harshest shame.
If cells produce love so brightly vernal
Then may those cells prove to be eternal!

66.

I thank you for giving me my poems,
For I never before you wrote like this.
I want these more than all other totems
To stand for me after I taste death's kiss.
My legacy of thirty years is lack.
It is dry and unproud, sad and without.
When I leave this life, I won't have to pack,
Since my accomplishments are but a drought.
Nevertheless, I still have this writing
That continues to be inspired by you.
Now introspection feels not as biting.
There's hope to make my legacy anew.
So thanks again for giving me this gift.
Even writing this gave my soul a lift.

67.

I enjoyed a luxurious meal's hour
Until I suddenly sensed your absence.
Then the finest delicacies went sour,
The meal becoming a pointless expense.
I realized you're more than icing or spice
But the essential nutrition of life.
Some grant the strength of sugar – you, of rice.
Some are cut easily – you need a knife.
Therefore, your absence is like starvation,
Starvation that does not kill but endures.
It's my heart's drought – your presence, hydration,
Hydration that not just maintains but cures.
As the nose and eye embrace the canna
So the heart covets you, loving manna.

68.

I write like this, as no one hears me speak.
Rhyming metaphors seem my whole know-how.
When I try to be clear, it's heard as Greek.
Closeness with others it does not allow.
Oh, to talk plainly with them, face to face!
To know and be known by some friendly souls.
To understand them and live at their pace,
To sound human and not like ancient scrolls.
Even poems can't express some ideas.
Some can only be lived, and felt, and breathed.
I wish I could describe her as she is,
But to me, her true self will remain sheathed.
Though knowledge of others I dare not claim,
I believe that all of us cry the same.

69.

When space itself feels made of coarsest stone,
And when I hiss at the chance to revel,
When no one and nothing feels like my own,
Then I have what ancients called a devil.
My arms' veins become as angry vipers.
My face becomes unrecognizable.
The airy outdoors feels full of snipers.
To drive becomes far from advisable.
I feel doomed to fight myself for others
And their threatening, demanding standard.
I devolve when faced with falsest brothers
And thus become worse than what they slandered.
The highest fear is not, "My life, he'll steal,"
But that when I am he, then I am real.

70.

There are things I know but will not believe
About myself, for I've chosen feeling
Over truth – to be wrong but not bereave,
To allow false fact to cause real healing.
There's an unspoken feeling that cripples
So much even the songwriters flee it.
When the pain of angry sadness triples,
Then exists shame and fear others see it.
Shame blares its horn into my inner ears,
Saying you left either scared or mocking
(That I caused you painful or scorning tears),
And that now you've gone to others talking.
Shame makes terror beyond a villain's grin,
For in shame, the villain lives on my skin.

71.

When the body breaks, there is a blood pour.
So then, when the mind breaks, there comes 'mind-blood.'
Like mind, it is unseen; but like red gore,
It shocks and frightens and spreads like a flood.
The pained psyche is a contagious hurt-
On more than one it demands a high toll.
As a violent brawl can stain a white shirt,
So savage tones contort the peaceful soul.
One shout, curse, obscenity leads to more.
Each victim becomes the next one's torment
Until chains of victims could pack a store
Even if nobody had ill intent.
So rather than being strangers' stressor,
Aim to make their brooding all the lesser.

72.

In looking back on these last four or five,
I feel the old need to apologize.
When writing with the thought of love, I thrive.
Rhymes come quickly, and the brain barely tries;
But sometimes I want to write of bad things,
And maybe I shouldn't burden readers
With therapeutic work in my mood swings,
For they come here as eaters, not feeders.
I've made my choice: darkness shall be discussed.
Not all darkness is comprised of evils.
Many guiltless things spark fear or disgust,
Like the thunder, fire, serpents, weevils.
Still, I see a clear difference in my work
When these dark emotions begin to lurk.

73.

Beauty comprises your atoms' atoms-
In this case, the parts resemble the whole-
And that beauty spreads past what man fathoms.
If blue stars are cold, then you are a troll.
As light needs a star to get emitted,
Nature's beauties are just your emissions,
So when against human art you're pitted,
Your natural fells all aestheticians.
And just as earth is hottest at its core,
Nature's glamor looks best at its center.
Though there's no nat'ral center to search for,
There's you. So says love's experimenter.
From tiniest quantum to vast galactic,
All beauty but yours is anticlimactic

74.

I am not reminded of you when sad.
Present sorrow connects me with mem'ry
Of past partners selfish and evil-clad
With cannon lungs and hearts so leathery.
Therefore, sorrow is a true time machine
And means of resurrecting the deceased,
But unlike Christ's resurrection serene,
Sorrow performs as the devil's high priest.
Now, the grass in late sunlight and calm breeze
Are things that do remind me of your touch.
Autumn's apples, bloomings, and colored trees
Reach deep in me and find whom I love much.
While sorrow digs up graves of evils past,
Happy times revive you, brightest contrast!

75.

Today I walked by a tall evergreen
And thought, *"I'd love to share with her its shade.*

She'd make this rustic spot still more serene
And cool my rage with mental lemonade."

If heaven varies by each person's want,
I know just how my side of it should look:
Her love would be my heavn'ly restaurant
As we'd hike each forest and swim each brook.
That tree today helped me realize something:
I need not win a war to feel divine,
Nor eat the dinners of the richest king.
Just let me sit with her under a pine.
And I suspect more random things I see
Will remind me of her, or so I plea.

76.

Each poet, it seems, writes of sun and moon
When talking love. I've thought of this of late-
How I'd use these words to make a love tune-
And now, at last, here's what I have to state:
My love resembles neither moon nor sun.
Moon has beauty while very far away,
But *her* beauty's better closer. Outdone
Is moon, who's gone from shining white to gray!
Sun's too often not around when wanted
And then, when arrived, is overbearing.
With *her*, love had never to be hunted
Yet knew its bounds, my privacy sparing.
I won't call her my sun and moon too fast,
For now I see clearly such a contrast.

77.

Childhood can return with but a smell-
If not events, then the feelings thereof.
A whiff of chocolate can summon past hell
Or make me young again for my young love.
And now my grown-up love has made her way
Into my past, for nostalgic fragrance
Brought up feelings mixed with her just today.
And she's welcome, for that joy she'll enhance.
I did not expect I would find her there
In my childhood's odors familiar.
If only the real she and I could share
My real complete timeline: are, will be, were.
It seems all things can be inspiration
To love her without equivocation.

78.

"There is no rejection here," says heaven.
"There is no one who will dismiss or scorn."
For rejection is the toughest leaven
To turn a hopeful, cheery soul forlorn.
Yet there needs to be the right to refuse,
Though that will not lessen the blow for us.
There's no excuse needed for one to choose
And no excuse for responding with fuss.
Oh, but what joy always to be adored!
If this impossibility were real!
To speak my full mind and make no one bored,
A fantasy both tempting and surreal.
It's all right to deny and be denied,
As well as to cry and cause to have cried.

79.

You are luxury and necessity-
Both need and want to me at the same time.
For now, there is no need to be witty-
I'll express this with rhymes not worth a dime.
It's better to be wanted than needed.
An irksome boss calls when I must be had,
And that state is sought by the conceited.
I wish you'd freely choose me as comrade.
But you need not know nor fear the diff'rence,
For, as I said, you have acquired both.
Before, to know love was as a sixth sense,
But now I am so sure I'd swear an oath.
You serve, again, as both water and wine,
The things in life both essential and fine.

80.

You are, indeed, like things I've seen before,
But these things were not seen with fleshly eyes.
They were seen with mind, as in dreams and lore
Or feelings felt when watching a sunrise.
You can say I saw you first with desire,
That is, with imagination and hope.
Then you came clothed in fleshly attire,
And my eyes perceived as though cleaned with soap:
"This is one for whom ancient poets longed,
The sort who inspires each culture's fine arts,
The wisdom for which great thinkers were wronged,
And who makes brave each country's soldiers' hearts!"
Now I know for sure that some truth lies in myth.
You come not from, but from you comes, the wordsmith.

81.

There's much others do far better than you,
Like corrupting, betraying, deceiving.
You are quite inept at making me blue,
And it's beyond you to be bereaving.
You have no idea how to ruin days,
And it's clear you never learned to annoy.
You're incompetent at blocking sun rays
Or robbing other people of their joy.
Whoever taught you to be envious?
Where did you learn the art of feeling spite?
You failed the test of being devious
And know nothing of making wrong from right.
And so, you get an F in meanness class
And a zero percent in all things crass.

82.

Great strength can be contained in tiny things,
As God, it seems, can be incarnated,
The use of atoms vast destruction brings,
And from a dot, a cosmos created!
I too am small, yet such a container
Of enormous power: that of great love.
To make my point again even plainer,
It's as Holy Spirit fleshed in a dove.
I often fear it will-defying strengths,
But ultimately, it's life-affirming.
It compels me to go to further lengths,
While my good health and safety confirming.
If a spark can make a conflagration,
Then I can love beyond time's duration.

83.

They say not to look for God eyes sky-ward,
Since the divine shines in my neighbor's face.
In the same way, you can be most assured
That in each person's smile, I see your trace.
When other people sneer or bear their teeth,
There, I see not one small atom like yours.
You are to them as rainforest to heath.
You are to ugliness as fun to chores.
In voice tones too, I hear your soft presence
Or lack thereof. In shouting, none of you,
Not a speck of your soul's iridescence.
Only in tender tones do you shine through.
Still, the good in others gives but a bare
And fuzzy sketch of you, oh one so rare.

84.

Why, when I touch wine, it turns to water?
While others, it seems, turn mud to gold,
I take fortunes and turn them to fodder,
Kept from mansions, lest I make of them mold.
Others' success is not inspiration
Unless I have my own to boast about.
Otherwise, their win is my frustration,
And then I feel ashamed because I pout.
But then I recall having touched treasures-
In the form of my love – that did *not* rot;
And there are no treasures finer than hers.
Hence, I curb anger and am less distraught.
Herein I see the wiser perspective:
I'll have the time we spent so long I live.

85.

I deeply wish that I could write music
To sing and play originals for you.
Instead, you bear my humor not-so-slick
And conversations that I fear bore you.
I hear such wonders from others' spirits
And envy their romantic skillfulness,
For I know I cannot match their merits,
No matter my exerted willfulness.
And I hate that piano's reluctance
To give me something to give to you, hon.
Trying to penetrate it like a lance
Did nothing at all – that stubborn wanton!
But I have gratitude for this at least:
I can give you berries, though not a feast.

86.

One of the litany of litanies
Of fine and admirable attributes
You have in overflowing quantities
Is to make me want to bear better fruits.
You don't follow the rule of one spoiled
Apple to the barrel, as your charming
Presence spreads good health and is not soiled
By boorish brutes who delight in harming.
You are the one sweet apple who makes good
All those who are otherwise bruised or stale.
You're a strong pillar amongst rotted wood,
Holding and supporting us like a nail.
You are a plague of health ever spreading,
Ever helpful, warm, and better getting.

87.

Flying, I was not happy to be close
To heaven but sad I was far from you.
I did not find the sun's realm grandiose,
But had you been there, you'd have changed my view.
All the beauty in the world is darkness
Until you, my light, make it come to life.
Just your presence transforms barren starkness
To divine oases with wonders rife.
To share with you some cheap cotton candy
Means more to me than basking in the clouds.
I'll pass private island beaches sandy
To trudge with you through rain in city crowds.
Wherever my flesh might travel by plane,
You always ride first class within my brain.

88.

You have changed a lot from my little elf
But not in losing your essential traits.
You have become more of and like yourself,
A good change happening at fastest rates.
You're not getting different but more the same,
And that is something glorious to see;
And your age will never prove cause for shame,
Even beyond the bristlecone pine tree.
And how do I know you won't change for worse?
It is a knowing that comes from trusting.
Your soul will not suffer an old age curse,
Nor shall your soft beauty endure rusting.
You are not constant like an ancient star
But grow more into the marvel you are.

89.

Because of you, I crave no nostalgia.
Carefree childhood joys have been replaced
With something better than any gala,
And that's your presence, with which I was graced.
Amen, the stress and frustrations of life
When grown can scrape the soul like sandpaper
And, in just one day, gut hope like a knife,
Making us long for days that felt safer.
Yet I would not trade in this lack of youth,
As in youth, there was no you to adore,
So even while slowly turning uncouth,
I admit I prefer this age far more.
Perhaps this is, to me, your greatest feat:
To cause youthful joys willingly to fleet.

90.

You are nothing like the moon or black holes.
The former just reflects another's light.
Black holes steal light, craving darkness like moles,
But you share your own, making less each plight
That I experience. You make me lose
Interest in astronomy. For how
Can celestial marvels fill your shoes
Or command from me the same humble bow?
What galaxy ever taught me to love?
Which nebula made of me a good man
Who longs to embrace rather than to shove?
Where were they when my most desperate tears ran?
Let space expand as far as it wishes.
To be near you is still most auspicious.

91.

Your almost supernatural beauty
Is something I must not ever forget;
So I already fear senility,
Which is, to my happiness, the worst threat,
Despite how far from me it leers and lurks.
To have a mind without your face in it-
What sorrow! And to forget your kind works-
Red hell! Such thoughts grab my soul and skin it!
To imagine this is like recalling
Where and in what form I was before birth.
It's the feeling of eternal falling,
The thought of non-being's darkness and dearth.
No. Let's now forget about forgetting,
Return to earth, ignore thoughts upsetting.

92.

I can't deny entry into my mind
This awful feeling from a foul neighbor,
Someone whose heart was covered with a rind
And quickly cut mine as with a saber;
So now that I have failed at ignoring,
I must succeed in accepting, bearing.
I wish my brain were much worse at storing
Such things as other people's eyes glaring
And their voices blaring, especially
When I prove otherwise so forgetful.
Why do happy facts not stay so freshly
Engrained? Why just those that make me fretful?
But wait – there *is* one such good fact always
Recalled: you shared with me some of your days.

93.

Whenever I am in your strong presence
I am at your mercy. To answer no
To a queen is difficult for peasants,
And when she's beloved, it's all the more so.
A heartless power's easy to reject.
The thrill of conquering grave injustice!
But to displease you is cause for regret-
The feeling that I have behaved amiss.
The adored inspire obedience
Better than the greatest terrifier,
So when the devil demands obeisance,
Those who know you will shout, "I stand by her."
I should be grateful you demand little.
Otherwise, I should prove very brittle.

94.

I know that the windy caress I felt
Outside today was not you, but I want
To pretend it was. It made my stress melt
As you did, making me feel not so gaunt
And tired. It both cooled and warmed somehow
At once, in the same way you both relaxed
And excited. Thus would you swiftly plow
Through all my stress with benefits untaxed.
If only your handiness and caring
Were as free and widely dispersed as wind.
Then there'd be no chance of me despairing,
No chance I'd look at my life and rescind.
But as there is no point in grabbing air,
I know it's best to move on from this flare.

95.

If Christ could not be recognized as God,
Of course not everyone sees your beauty.
Remember how many are like Nimrod
In being hopelessly proud and snooty.
While I hate to see you disappointed,
I trust fully you're strong enough for it.
Saul scorned David for being anointed,
And when you face your Sauls, you'll endure it.
And when upset, let me be Barnabas
To you, who is son of encouragement.
When they talk of you with insults and cuss,
Know that all they do is misrepresent.
There were many kings but only one Esther,
And as with you, no wicked one could best her.

96.

I've discovered a tenth beatitude:
"Happy are those who spend a day with you."
Happy they are and full of gratitude.
Even on your worst day, how could one rue
Time engulfed in your health-filled ambiance?
Next to you, one receives well-being free.
As love is brought out by being in France,
Sitting by you treats the soul tenderly.
You are the meaning of quality time.
I don't have better things to do, places
To be, or people to meet, and so I'm
Granting you access to all my spaces.
I hide myself from others in the shade
But give to you my lifetime to invade.

97.

If the belief in reincarnation
Is true, then your last life must have excelled
In all virtues. My last: depravation.
Yours: a spectacular to have beheld;
And your next will surely glow with luster,
Perhaps even beyond this fleshly plane.
It would take all virtue I can muster
An incarnation like yours to obtain.
Though, like all, you have your many trials,
Your mind and frame still prove you are gifted;
And your response to them put you miles
Ahead of others from whom you're sifted.
If our lifetimes stay ever repeating,
What joy to make new our ev'ry meeting!

98.

If you were the only woman on earth,
Your beauty would be no reason for awe.
In the face of many, you prove your worth.
There is not one with whom you call a draw.
Others, also, can prove bright and witty,
Which is what makes your mind stand up so high.
Among many a populous city,
You are Tokyo, Delhi, and Shenghai.
Some people's hearts are as large as Neptune,
Uranus, or Saturn, but yours towers
Over Jupiter. That's why I'm immune
To others' dazzling charms and powers.
So yes, many can make me fast impressed,
Which only serves to prove you are most blessed.

99.

I hate this room, which contains no loved ones.
It contains only me, who is no such
Loved one of mine. I'm like unwilling nuns
Or captured wildlife forced into a hutch;
But outside's no different, as my jail cell
Is not made with walls or bars, not truly,
Nor is it imposed on me as a hell
To punish some behavior unruly.
See the confinement of ineptitude-
The inability to understand.
When others' wishes constantly elude,
Then from their presence constantly I'm banned.
The distances of many pinch like crabs,
But hers is the distance that deeply stabs.

100.

To write poems, I give you this learning:
Do not focus on what others have said
But gaze inward and hear your own yearning,
Ignore not that for which your soul has bled.
From others, we must learn the rudiments:
The letters and words of our different tongues,
But from there, we learn from our lives' events,
The days that milk song and scream from our lungs.
Let the words rise from inside on their own
Without regard for the need to adhere;
And if she has become your cornerstone,
Hide no feeling but let that truth appear.
Such was the truth for me.